C000045344

WHY ARMENIA SHOULD BE FREE

ARMENIA'S RÔLE IN THE PRESENT WAR

BY

Dr. G. PASDERMADJIAN

(ARMEN GARO)

EX-DEPUTY FROM ERZEROUM IN THE OTTOMAN PARLIAMENT
FORMER COMMANDER OF THE SECOND BATTALION OF THE ARMENIAN
VOLUNTEERS ON THE CAUCASIAN FRONT
REPRESENTATIVE IN AMERICA OF ARMENIAN NATIONAL COUNCIL OF THE
CAUCASUS.

WITH AN INTRODUCTION BY

GEORGE NASMYTH, Ph. D.

FORMER PRESIDENT OF THE CENTRAL COMMITTEE OF THE INTERNATIONAL
FEDERATION OF STUDENTS
SECRETARY OF THE MASSACHUSETTS JOINT COMMITTEE
FOR A LEAGUE OF FREE NATIONS

ILLUSTRATED

BOSTON
HAIRENIK PUBLISHING COMPANY
1918.

WRITTEN AT WASHINGTON, D. C., OCTOBER, 1918.
ALL RIGHTS RESERVED

Published, December, 1918

JUN 7   1928
QP.

The Blanchard Printing Co.
Boston   Massachusetts.

In the interest of creating a more extensive selection of rare historical book reprints, we have chosen to reproduce this title even though it may possibly have occasional imperfections such as missing and blurred pages, missing text, poor pictures, markings, dark backgrounds and other reproduction issues beyond our control. Because this work is culturally important, we have made it available as a part of our commitment to protecting, preserving and promoting the world's literature. Thank you for your understanding.

DR. G. PASDERMADJIAN
(Armen Garo)

TO THOSE WHO WERE MARTYRED

AND

TO THOSE WHO DIED ON THE FIELD OF BATTLE

FOR THE LIBERATION OF ARMENIA

CONTENTS

INTRODUCTION

ARMENIA has become a touchstone of victory in the great war for freedom and humanity.

If Armenia is granted national independence it will mean that in the making of the peace treaty the forces of democracy and human progress have triumphed over the forces of imperialism and short-sighted reaction. It will mean that in the future the rights of the small nations are to be recognized as well as those of the great. It will mean that international justice is to be the foundation of the new world order. The triumph of the principle that is involved will mean that the war has been won because its moral aims have been achieved.

But if the Armenians were to be thrust back under the yoke of Turkey, it would mean that injustice, massacre and atrocity are to be permanent features of the world of the future. It would mean that the justice-loving nations of the world will prepare for inevitable conflicts that are to come. It would mean that the war which was fought to end war has been lost.

National independence for Armenia will mean that the old order of secret intrigue and orthodox diplomacy has given way to a new order of open democratic diplomacy, based on the self-determination of nations and the principles of international justice. It will mean that the peace which ends this war will be a democratic peace, a peace of the peoples, a peace that will last. It will mean that imperialistic aims, secret treaties and selfish greedy interests have given way before the conception of a world organized for righteousness and permanent peace.

National independence for Armenia will mean that the Balance of Power, which has always considered the subject nations of Turkey as mere pawns in a diplomatic game, has been replaced by a League of Free Nations opening the way towards a world federation and the parliament of man. It will mean that the old chaos of international anarchy is to be replaced by a new world order in which peoples and nations shall be free to live their own lives, to speak their own language, to worship in their

1

own religion and to develop their own civilization, in the fullest friendship and democratic co-operation with the other free nations of mankind.

National independence for Armenia is a touchstone of victory because it will mean that mankind has come to recognize that there is a moral law in the world, which applies to nations as well as to individuals. It will mean the overthrow of imperialism, militarism and the philosophy of force. It will mean an invaluable extension of the principle of democracy in the world. It will mean that the way will be open to develop the great highway between Europe and Asia amid political conditions of a stable and durable peace. It will mean that mankind can proceed to cultivate again the valleys of the Tigris and the Euphrates and that once more after centuries of desolation this region will become one of the garden spots of the earth.

What should be the boundaries of the new Armenian nation? I have before me Stanford's Linguistic Map of Europe, a map based upon the most careful scientific research and conscientious scholarship. This map shows the area in which the Armenian speaking population is dominant as extending to Adana and Alexandretta on the Mediterranean, almost to the Black Sea near Trebizond, to Tiflis in the Caucasus Mountains and to Lake Urmia near the western boundary of Persia on the East.

At the edges this Armenian territory shades over into regions occupied by Turks and Kurds. In the interest of international justice and permanent peace in the future, the boundaries of the new Armenia ought to be extended as far as the Armenian race extends as an important element of the population, because the Armenians have proved their capacity for self-government even under the almost impossible conditions of Turkish misrule, while Turks and Kurds have again and again proved incapable of governing themselves, much less of governing others. The hope for toleration of racial minorities, which is the indispensable condition for peace in areas of mixed population, would be many times greater in a government by the Armenians than in a government by Turks and Kurds.

Armenia is a touchstone of victory in this war because, unlike Belgium, it lies so far beyond the range of accurate news reports and the limelight of public opinion, that it is likely to be overlooked unless a settlement is approached in a new spirit of international justice. The horrors of the

Armenian massacres have been so unendurable that many people have had to try to escape from thinking about Armenia in order to keep their sanity in the midst of such wholesale horror. But oblivion is no remedy for the problem of Armenia and the world of the future will not be safe for democracy or for anything else unless Armenia and the problem which it represents is permanently solved in the Peace Conference. I do not believe that any indemnities or annexations of territories or any imperialistic gain of this war is worth the life of a single American soldier, but I do believe that only by giving Armenia its independence, by establishing the principle of international justice, of which Armenia is a concrete example, and by creating a League of Free Nations as the basis of the new world order, will we be enabled to say that the sacrifices of these young men shall not have been in vain. Thus Armenia becomes the touchstone of victory in this great war for freedom and humanity.

GEORGE NASMYTH.

BOSTON, MASS.
DECEMBER 12, 1918.

TRANSLATOR'S PREFACE

DR. PASDERMADJIAN, the author of this pamphlet, is a native of Erzeroum, and a member of a family which, both in the past and in the present, has been an object of barbarous persecution at the hands of the Turks. When the Russians in 1829 captured Erzeroum for the first time, 96,000 Armenians, with the encouragement of the Russian government, left that city and the outlying villages with the Russian army, and emigrated towards the Caucasus, where they founded three new cities, Alexandropol, Akhalkalak, and Akhaltsikh. Only 300 Armenian families remained in Erzeroum, refusing to leave their homes, even in face of the Turkish despotism. Among these was the Pasdermadjian family.

In 1872 the Turkish government had Khatchatour Pasdermadjian killed, simply because he was a well-to-do and influential Armenian, and, therefore, undesirable. In 1877 during the Russo-Turkish war, the Pasdermadjian family was subjected to the basest kind of persecution by the Turkish government, which still owes the Pasdermadjians 36,000 Turkish *liras* ($180,000), the value of a quantity of wheat wrested from them by the military authorities. During those same hostilities, taking advantage of the war conditions, the Turkish government planned to hang Haroutiun Pasdermadjian, on the ground that he was in communication with the Russian army; but he was saved through the intervention of the British consul. When the Russian army occupied Erzeroum in 1878, the Pasdermadjians naturally gave a very hospitable reception to the two Armenian Generals, Loris Melikoff and Lazareff. After learning of the family's history, Loris Melikoff asked Haroutiun Pasdermadjian to emigrate to the Caucasus. He promised to bring the influence of the Russian government to bear on Turkey and to claim the family's extensive real estate and various sums of money which the Turkish government owed them. But Haroutiun Pasdermadjian refused the kind offer, saying that he could not leave the country which contained his martyred father's grave. When the Russians, in accordance with the terms of the Berlin Treaty, were forced to evacuate

5

Erzeroum, the Turks came back and began anew to persecute the Pasdermadjians in every possible way. In 1890 the Armenians of Erzeroum made a protest against Turkish despotism, and demanded to have the reforms promised in the Berlin Treaty carried out. The first bullet fired by the Turkish soldiers during those disturbances was aimed at Haroutiun Pasdermadjian; but he was saved through the heroism of a group of young Armenians. In the massacres of 1895, the Pasdermadjians were again attacked by an armed Turkish mob, but were saved from plunder and murder through the stubborn resistance of all the members of the household, including the servants. Afterwards, three members of the family, Hovhannes, Tigrane, and Setrak, were imprisoned for a long time as revolutionists. In reality, they were imprisoned simply because they had not allowed themselves to be slaughtered like sheep by the Turkish mob. In February, 1915, when the present Turkish government began its organized slaughters to eliminate the Armenians from the world, the first victim in Erzeroum was Setrak Pasdermadjian, because he was an influential Armenian and had had the courage several times to protest against the unlawful acts of the government. The remnants of this numerous and ancient Armenian family are now scattered throughout Mesopotamia.

The author of this booklet, Garegin Pasdermadjian, is the son of Haroutiun Pasdermadjian and the grand-son of Khatchatour Efendi. He was born in 1873, and received his elementary education at the Sanasarian College of Erzeroum, being one of its first graduates (1891). In 1894 he went to France and studied agriculture in the college at Nancy, intending to return and develop the lands belonging to his family according to the modern agricultural methods of Europe, and in that way give a practical lesson to the Armenian peasants. He had hardly begun his course when the great massacres of 1895 revolutionized the plans of the younger generation of Armenian students. Out of the 26 young Armenians at the University of Nancy, four, Sarkis Srentz, Haik Thirakian, Max Zevrouz, and Garegin Pasdermadjian, left their studies and returned to participate in the effort at vengeance which the Armenian Revolutionary Dashnaktzoutiun (Federation) had decided to organize in Constantinople. In 1896, Garegin Pasdermadjian and Haik Thirakian, under their assumed names of Armen Garo and Hratch respectively, took part in the seizure of the Ottoman Bank. This European institution, with its 154 inmates and 300 million francs ($60,000,000) of capital, remained in the hands of the Armenian revolutionists for fourteen hours as a pledge that the European ambassadors should immediately stop the Armenian massacre in Constantinople and give assurances that the reforms guaranteed to the Armenians in the Treaty of Berlin should be carried out. On behalf of the six great powers, signatories to the Berlin Treaty, the chief interpreter of the Russian embassy, Mr. Maximoff, made a gentleman's agreement with the young Armenian revolutionists to fulfill their demands. Trusting to Mr. Maximoff's word of honor, the Armenians left Constantinople. But immediately after their departure, the massacres were resumed with more intensity, while the reforms have remained a dead letter to this day. Such were international morals in 1895.

After these events Garegin Pasdermadjian returned to Europe to continue his unfinished studies. Mr. Hanoteau, however, the French foreign minister at that time, would not allow the Armenians who had been connected with this affair to remain in France, so young Pasdermadjian went to Switzerland and studied the natural sciences at the University of Geneva. In 1900 he completed his course and received the degree of Doctor of Science. Unable to return to Turkish Armenia, as was his desire, Dr. Pasdermadjian went to the Caucasus and settled at Tiflis in 1901. There he opened the first chemical laboratory, for the purpose of investigating the rich mines of that region.

National events, however, prevented him from pursuing his research work. Having been a member of the responsible body of the Armenian Revolutionary Dashnaktzoutiun (Federation) since 1896, he took part in all the movements which aimed to protect the moral and physical well being of the Armenian people from Turkish and Russian despotism. For example, in 1905, when the Caucasian Tartars, with the approval of the Russian government, began to massacre the Armenians in divers parts of the Caucasus, Dr. Pasdermadjian became a member of the Committee created by the Armenian Revolutionary Dashnaktzoutiun (Federation) to organize defence work among the Armenian people. In November of the same year, when the Armeno-Tartar hostilities began right in Tiflis, under the very nose of the Russian administration, he was entrusted with the command of the Armenian volunteers to protect Tiflis and its environs. During the seven-day struggle which took place in the streets of Tiflis, 500 Armenian volunteers faced nearly 1400 armed Tartars, and drove them back with heavy losses.

The situation in the Caucasus was almost normal, and Dr. Pasdermadjian and his idealistic colleagues were about to resume their main object, —to carry arms and ammunition from the Caucasus to the Turkish Armenians in order to prepare them for self-defense,—when the Turkish revolution came in 1908. The Armenians in Erzeroum, as well as the party to which he was a member, telegraphed to Dr. Pasdermadjian and strongly urged him to become their candidate in the coming elections for Representative to the Ottoman Parliament. After seven years of professional studies, Dr. Pasdermadjian had been able to create for himself in the Caucasus a life fairly prosperous financially. He had just secured the right to develop a copper mine, and was about to work it in partnership with a large company. His business required that he should stay in the Caucasus to continue his successful enterprise, but he yielded to the moral pressure of his comrades and left his personal affairs to go to Constantinople as a deputy from Erzeroum.

During his four years in Constantinople as a deputy, Dr. Pasdermadjian devoted his entire time to better the economic conditions of the Armenian vilayets, and especially worked for the railroad bill, of which he was the real author, but which was known to the public as Chester's bill. Its main object was to build railroads as soon as possible in those vilayets of Armenia which were considered to be Russia's future possessions. For that reason neither France nor Germany wished to undertake it, lest they should arouse the enmity of Russia. Another fundamental object was to build those lines with American capital, which would make it possible to counteract the Russo-Franco-German policies and financial intrigues, for the benefit of the Armenian people. But in spite of all his efforts, Dr. Pasdermadjian was unable to overcome the German opposition in Constantinople, although, as the outcome of the struggle in connection with that bill, two ministers of public works were forced to resign their post. Both of the ministers were absolute German agents under the name of Turkish ministers. It may also be worth mentioning that during his four years at Constantinople as a deputy from Erzeroum, at three different times, Talaat Bey (who became the butcher of the Armenian people in 1915), on behalf of the

"Committee of Union and Progress," offered the portfolio of public works to Dr. Pasdermadjian, as the most competent man for the post. Dr. Pasdermadjian, however, refused these proposals, for the simple reason that he did not wish to compromise in any way with the leaders of the Turkish government, as long as they continued their chauvinistic and anti-Armenian policy.

In the parliamentary elections of 1914, the "Committee of Union and Progress" used every means to defeat the election of Dr. Pasdermadjian in Erzeroum. On account of this attitude of the Turks, all the Armenian inhabitants of the Erzeroum vilayet refused to take part in the last elections. This intense opposition of the Turks to the candidacy of Dr. Pasdermadjian was due to the fact that he had taken too active a part in 1913 in the conferences held for the consideration of the Armenian reforms, and especially because, while parliamentary elections were going on in Turkish Armenia during April, 1914, he was in Paris and Holland, as the delegate of the Armenian Revolutionary Dashnaktzoutiun (Federation), to meet the inspectors general who were invited to carry out the reforms in Turkish Armenia.

In the autumn of 1914, a month and a half before the beginning of Turco-Russian hostilities, Dr. Pasdermadjian went to the Caucasus on a special mission, and joined the committee which had been appointed by the Armenian National Council of the Caucasus to organize the Armenian volunteer movement. In November of the same year, when the Russo-Turkish war had begun, he accompanied the second battalion of the Armenian volunteers, as the representative of the executive committee of Tiflis, to prepare the local inhabitants of Turkish Armenia for self-defence, as the Russian army was about to advance into the captured territories of that country. On November 14 the second battalion of the Armenian volunteers engaged in battle for the first time, near Bayazid, with the Turkish soldiers and the Kurds. In the course of a bloody combat which lasted twenty-four hours, Dro, the brave commander of the battalion, was seriously wounded, and Dr. Pasdermadjian was forced immediately to take his place. From that day to March of the following year, he remained at the head of that battalion, and led it into eleven battles in the neighborhood of Alashkert, Toutakh, and Malashkert, until Dro recovered and returned to resume the command. In the summer of 1915, Dr. Pasdermadjian (again as a representative of the executive committee of Tiflis) went to Van. He was there when the people migrated en masse to the Caucasus (when the Russian army was forced to retreat to the old Russo-Turkish frontiers) and shared their untold hardships.

In the spring of 1917, when the Russian Revolution turned all the defence work of the Caucasus up-side down, Dr. Pasdermadjian, with Dr. Zavrieff, was sent from the Caucasus to Petrograd to negotiate with the temporary Russian government concerning Caucasian affairs. From Petrograd he left for America in June of the same year as the representative of the Armenian National Council of Tiflis and as the special Envoy of His Holiness the Catholicos of all the Armenians, to lay before the American public and government the sorrows of the Armenian people with the view of winning their sympathy and protection for the indisputable rights of Armenia. He is still acting in that capacity with all the energy at his command. His last effort has been the preparation of this pamphlet, in which the reader will find a part of these biographical facts under his assumed name of Armen Garo.

A word or two more about this booklet, which has been written in the nick of time.

The critical days in the spring of this year are over, and the complete victory of the Allies and of the United States has been won. "The day is not very far," in the words of the writer, "when . . . the representatives of all the nations of the world,—guilty or just,—are to receive their punishment or reward . . " It is the purpose of this pamphlet to demonstrate beyond any shadow of doubt, with most authentic facts, that Armenia has fulfilled her duty to the allied cause in full measure (and suffered untold sacrifices in doing so), and, therefore, is entitled to her just claims as an Independent Armenia.

One other purpose the writer had in view in writing this booklet: to make the great and generous American public realize that Armenians are not an anaemic and unaggressive people, with no fighting blood in their veins; that the Armenians have not been butchered like sheep, but, on the contrary, have fought most bravely and resisted most stubbornly the savage attacks of the Turks whenever they had an opportunity.

If the translation can possibly convey the spirit of the original, the sustained eloquence and suppressed emotion with which the author pleads the cause of his unfortunate but brave people, should be intensely effective because they are not mere words, but are based on actual, real, undeniable facts, and are the expression of a soul wholly dedicated to a sacred cause.

A. T.

Cambridge, Mass.
December, 1918.

WHY ARMENIA SHOULD BE FREE
ARMENIA'S RÔLE IN THE PRESENT WAR

"The interest of the weakest is as sacred as the interest of the strongest."

PRESIDENT WILSON.

New York, Sept. 27, 1918.

A seventy-year old Armenian priest leading the volunteers
to the battlefield.

WHY ARMENIA SHOULD BE FREE
ARMENIA'S RÔLE IN THE PRESENT WAR

IN the early days of August, 1914, when civilized nations took up arms against the German aggression, only three of the smaller nations of Europe and the Near East had the courage, from the very first days of the war, to stand by the Allies without any bargaining or dickering, and they still stand at their posts on the ramparts, in spite of the immense sacrifices they have already made.

The first member of this heroic triad was brave Serbia, which was the first victim of Austrian aggression, and whose sons, after four years of heroic struggle, are about to regain their lost native land. The second member was little Belgium, whose three weeks of heroic resistance delayed the German advance of 1914 and enabled gallant France to crown with success the historic battle of the Marne. The third member of this heroic triad was the Armenian people, who for four years and without an organized government or a national army, played the same role in the Near East by preventing the Turco-German advance toward the interior of Asia as the Belgians played in the West by arresting the march of Germany toward Paris. The Armenians, however, paid a higher price to the God of War than either the Belgians or the Serbs. Out of four and one-quarter millions of Armenians living in Turkey and Russia at the beginning of the war, scarcely three millions remain at the present time. What were the conditions under which the Armenians sided with the Allies, and why were they forced to bear so great a sacrifice for their cause?

TURKISH AND RUSSIAN PROPOSALS TO THE ARMENIANS IN 1914.

In the beginning of this world conflagration, in 1914, both the Russian and the Turkish governments officially appealed to various Armenian national organizations with many promises in order to secure the active participation of the Armenians in the military operations against each other, the principal stage of which would be Armenia itself. Both

15

Turkey and Russia were very anxious to win the co-operation of the the Armenians, because, judging from their past experience, they were convinced that without such co-operation they would not be able to accomplish the much desired military successes on the Armenian plateau.

With such aims in view, Russia, through Count Varantzoff Dashkoff, informed the Armenian National Council (then in existence at Tiflis) that if the Armenians would unreservedly give their support to the Russian armies during the course of the war, Russia would grant autonomy to the six Armenian vilayets. The Russian Armenians, however, through bitter experience, knew very well what little practical value could be attached to the promises of Russian Czarism. During the course of the 19th century at three different times the Russians had made similar promises to the Armenians when they waged war with Turkey and Persia, and, although the self-sacrificing co-operation of the Russian Armenians enabled the Russians to capture the districts of Elizavetpol, Erivan and Kars in 1806, in 1828, and again in 1878, at the end of these wars their flattering promises to the Armenians were promptly forgotten. But this time the Armenians thought that Russia was not alone; the two great liberal nations of the West, France and England, were her Allies. After long and weighty consultation, with their hopes pinned on France and England, the Armenians resolved to aid the Russian armies in every possible way.

While Russian diplomacy was in the midst of these diplomatic negotiations at Tiflis, during the last days of August, 1914, a Turkish mission of twenty-eight members (the object of which was to organize a Pan-Islamic and a Pan-Turanian movement among all the races of the Near East against Russia and her Allies) left Constantinople for Armenia. The leaders of that mission were Omar Nadji Bey, Dr. Bahaeddin Shakir, and Lieutenant Hilmy, all of them very influential members of the "Committee of Union and Progress." The mission included representatives of all the Eastern races, such as the Kurds, Persians, Georgians, Chechens, Lezgies, Circassians, and the Caucasian Tartars, but not the Armenians. During those same days the annual Congress of the Armenian National Organization was in session at Erzeroum. In the name of the Turkish government the above mentioned mission appealed to the Armenian Organization with the following proposition:

Armenians of Van defending themselves against the Turkish and Kurdish raids in 1915.   The volunteers in their trenches.

"If the Armenians,—the Turkish as well as the Russian Armenians—would give active co-operation to the Turkish armies, the Turkish government under a German guarantee would promise to create after the war an autonomous Armenia (made up of Russian Armenia and the three Turkish vilayets of Erzeroum, Van, and Bitlis) under the suzerainty of the Ottoman Empire."

The Turkish delegates, in order to persuade the Armenians to accept this proposal, informed them also that they (the Turks) had already won the co-operation of the Georgians and the Tartars, as well as the mountaineers of the northern Caucasus, and therefore the noncompliance of the Armenians under such circumstances would be very stupid and fraught with danger for them on both sides of the boundary between Turkey and Russia. In spite of these promises and threats, the executive committee of the Dashnaktzoutiun (Federation) informed the Turks that the Armenians could not accept the Turkish proposal, and on their behalf advised the Turks not to participate in the present war, which would be very disastrous to the Turks themselves. The Armenian members of this parley were the well-known publicist, Mr. E. Aknouni, the representative from Van, Mr. A. Vramian, and the director of the Armenian schools in the district of Erzeroum, Mr. Rostom. Of these Mr. Aknouni and Mr. Vramian were treacherously killed a few months later for their audacious refusal of the Turkish proposals, while Mr. Rostom luckily escaped the murderous plots against his life.

The bold retort of the Armenians to the Turkish proposal mentioned above, intensely angered the Turks, and from that very day the extermination of the Armenians was determined upon by the Turkish government. And in reality, arrests and persecutions within the Armenian vilayets began in the early part of September, 1914, a month and a half before the commencement of the Russo-Turkish war. The speed of the persecutions gained greater momentum as the months rolled by and tens of villages in different parts of Armenia were subjected to fire and sword. In the district of Van alone, during February and March of 1915, twenty-four villages were razed to their foundations and their populations put to the sword. Early in April of the same year, they attempted the massacre of the inhabitants of the city of Van as well, but the Armenians took up arms, and, guided by their brave leader, Aram, defended their lives and property for a whole month, until the Armenian volunteers from Erivan with Russian soldiers came to the rescue and saved them from the impending doom. This resistance on the part of the inhabitants of Van gave the Turkish government a pretext to deport in June and July of the same year the entire Armenian population of Turkish Armenia, with the pretended intention of transporting them to Mesopotamia, but with the actual determination to exterminate them. Out of the million and a half of Armenians deported, scarcely 400,000 to 500,000 reached the sandy deserts of Syria and Mesopotamia, and most of these were women, old men, and children, who were subjected in those desolate regions to the mortal pangs of famine. More than a million defenceless Armenians were murdered at the hands of Turkish soldiers and Turkish mobs. The gang of robbers, headed by Talaat and Enver, resorted to this fiendish means to eliminate the Armenian question once for all, because the Armenians had had the courage to oppose their Pan-Turanian policies. The barbarities of Jenghiz Khan and Tamerlane pale in comparison with the savageries which were perpetrated against the Turkish Armenians in the summer of 1915 during this wholesale massacre organized by the Turkish government. Mr. Morgenthau, who was the American ambassador at Constantinople during those frightful months, has proclaimed all these atrocities by his authentic pen to the civilized nations. This was the price which the Armenian people paid within the boundaries of Turkey for refusing to aid the Turco-German policies.

Now let us see what positive services from a military point of view this same martyred people rendered to the allied cause on both sides of the Turco-Russian boundary line.

MILITARY SERVICES RENDERED BY THE ARMENIANS ON THE CAUCASIAN FRONT

In order to have an adequate comprehension of the events which took place on the Caucasian front, it would be well to bear in mind that all the peoples of Trans-Caucasia, including the Armenians, felt great enmity toward the government of the Czar, whose treatment of them in the past had been very tyrannical and very brutal. For this very reason, the Turco-German propaganda had easily won the sympathy of nearly 3,000,000 Tartars and 2,000,000 Georgians. The dream of the

Armenian volunteers of the Caucasus taking the oath of allegiance administered by the church dignitaries before leaving for the battlefield in October, 1914.

Tartars was to join the Ottoman Turks and re-establish the old great Tartar Empire, which was to extend from Constantinople to Samarkant, including all the lands of the Caucasus and Trans-Caspia, while the Georgians, through their alliance with the Turco-Germans, hoped to regain their lost independence in the western Caucasus. Only the 2,000,000 Armenians of the Caucasus were not influenced by the Turco-German propaganda, although they hated the Russian despotism as much as their neighbors. But, on the other hand, having very close acquaintance with the psychology of the Turkish race and with their ulterior aspirations, the Armenians had the political wisdom and courage to put aside their petty quarrels with Russian Czarism and throw in their lot with the allied cause.

These were the circumstances under which the mobilization of 1914 took place in the Caucasus. The Armenian reservists, about 160,000 in number, gladly responded to the call, for the simple reason that they were to fight the arch enemy of their historic race. Besides the regular soldiers, nearly 20,000 volunteers expressed their readiness to take up arms against the Turks. The Georgians, on the other hand, answered the call very reluctantly, and the Armenian-Georgian relations were greatly strained from the very beginning. The attitude of the Armenians toward the despotic Russian government was incomprehensible to the Georgians, who thought that, because the Armenians sided with Russia,—the oppressor of all the Caucasian races,—they must be unfriendly to the Georgians. Many Georgian young men crossed the border from Batoum, went to Trebizond, and prepared bands of volunteers under the leadership of Prince Abashizé in order to aid the Turks. As to the Tartars, not being subject to call, they assumed the role of spectators on the one hand, and on the other used every means to arm themselves, impatiently awaiting the arrival of the Turks. The great land-owners of the provinces of Erivan, Elizavetpol, and Baku began to accumulate enormous stores, and prepare a huge reserve of sugar and wheat. The price of one rifle, which was 100 rubles ($50), rose to 1500 rubles ($750). Through Persia, the Germans took to the Caucasus great sums of money in order to push forward the task of arming the Tartars from the very first days of the war. Great numbers of young Tartars went to Persia and joined the Turkish armies. And all this was carried on in broad daylight under the very eyes of the short-sighted Russian bureaucracy.

The Russian administration of the Caucasus was more concerned with the Armenian "danger" and had no time to pay attention to the Georgians and the Tartars. Was it not a fact that officially no Georgian or Tartar question was placed on the diplomatic table, whereas the Armenian question was there? And for that very reason, before the commencement of the Russo-Turkish hostilities, the second and third army corps of the Caucasian army, the majority of which were Armenians, were transferred to the German front and were replaced by Russian army corps. Moreover, out of the 20,000 Armenian volunteers who responded to the call, only 7,000 were given arms; the authorities objected that they had no rifles ready, while a few months later the same administration distributed 24,000 rifles to the Kurds in Persia and in the district of Van. It is needless to say that all the Armenian officers and generals were transferred to the Western front; only one Armenian general was left as a specimen on the entire Caucasian front, General Nazarbekoff, and he was transferred to Persia, away from the Armenian border. Under these trying conditions commenced the Russo-Turkish war and the Armenian-Russian co-operation on the Caucasian front in the autumn of 1914. But, in spite of this suspicious and crafty attitude assumed by the Russian administration, the Armenian inhabitants of the Caucasus spared nothing in their power for the success of the Russian armies. In the three main unsuccessful Turkish offensives the battalions of Armenian volunteers played a great role. Let us now see just what took place during those offensives.

The first serious Turkish offensive took place in the beginning of December, 1914, when Enver Pasha attempted to reach Tiflis by shattering the right wing of the Russian army. The Turkish "Napoleon" was anxious to connect his name with that great victory which seemed certain to his puny brain. And with that very purpose in view he boarded Goeben, the German cruiser, and left Constantinople, amid great demonstrations. He reached Erzeroum in three days, thanks to the German automobiles which were ready for him at different stops between Trebizond and the frontier. The offensive was planned with great care, and had great chances of success if all the three wings of the Turkish army had reached their objectives on time. Enver had under his command three army corps—the ninth, the tenth, and the

KERI   VARTAN   HAMAZASP

Commanders of Armenian volunteers; Keri, of the 4th battalion;
Hamazasp, of the 3rd battalion, and Vartan, of the
regiment of Ararat.

eleventh. The ninth army corps was to advance toward Ardahan by way of Olti and from there to march on Tiflis by way of Akhalkalag, when it should receive word that the tenth army corps had already captured Sarikamish and cut off the retreat of the Russian army of 60,000 men; while the eleventh army corps was to attack the centre of the Russian army near the frontier. The ninth army corps, in three days and without difficulty, reached Ardahan, where the local Moslem inhabitants assisted it in every possible way. The tenth army corps, during its march from Olti to Sarikamish, suffered a delay of twenty-four hours in the Barduz Pass, due to the heroic resistance of the fourth battalion of the Armenian volunteers which made up the Russian reserve. This delay of twenty-four hours enabled the Russians to concentrate a sufficient force around Sarikamish (which had been left entirely undefended) and thereby force back the ninth corps of the Turkish army. The Turks were so certain of the success of their plan that they had no transports with them and no extra supply of provisions. Opposite Sarikamish, where a battle was waged for three days and three nights, the Turks suffered a loss of 30,000 men, mostly due to cold rather than to the Russian arms. But if the Turkish army corps had reached Sarikamish twenty-four hours earlier, as was expected, it would have confronted only one battalion of Russian reserves, and that without artillery. This was the invaluable service rendered to the Russian army by the fourth battalion of the Armenian volunteers under the command of the matchless Keri. Six hundred Armenian veterans fell in the Barduz Pass, and at such a high price saved the 60,000 Russians from being taken prisoners by the Turks. This great service of the Armenians to the Russian army was announced at the time by Enver Pasha himself, when he returned to Constantinople immediately after his defeat. From that time on the government at Constantinople laid the blame of its defeat at the door of the Armenians, as a preliminary step in its preparation for the execution of its already-planned massacres of the Armenian people.

After their defeat at Sarikamish, the Turks attempted in April of 1915 to turn the extreme left wing of the Russian army by marching to Joulfa through Persia, and from there (in case of success) moving on to Baku, with the hope that the Tartar inhabitants of the eastern Caucasus would immediately join them and enable them to cut the only communicating line of railroad of the Russians, and thereby force the entire Russian army to retreat toward the northern Caucasus. The work of the intelligence department of the Turks was very well organized, especially as the Tartar and Georgian officers of the Caucasus rendered them invaluable services. The Turks knew very well that the Russians in Persia at that time had only one brigade of Russian troops under the command of the Armenian General Nazarbekoff and one battalion of Armenian volunteers scattered throughout Salmast and Urmia, while their own army was made up of one regular and well-drilled division of troops (sent especially from Constantinople) under the command of Khalil Bey and nearly 10,000 Kurds. Khalil Bey with his superior forces captured the city of Urmia in a few hours (taking prisoners nearly a thousand Russians) and victoriously marched on Salmast. Here took place one of the fiercest battles between the Armenians and the Turks. The first battalion of the Armenian volunteers, under the command of the veteran Andranik, strongly enforced in its trenches, repulsed the attacks of Khalil Bey for three days continuously, until the Russians, with the newly-arrived forces from the Caucasus, were able to put to flight the army of Khalil Bey. Thirty-six hundred Turkish soldiers lay dead before the Armenian trenches in the course of those three days.

In that very month of April, while Khalil Bey was confidently attempting, as we have seen, to surround the left wing of the Russian army in Persia, over in Van the Armenians had taken up arms in self-defence, and for one whole month were fighting another division of Turkish troops and thousands of Kurds until the first days of May, when three other battalions of Armenian volunteers, under the command of General Nikolaeff, came to the rescue, riding a distance of 250 kilometers (155 miles)—from Erivan to Van—in ten days. For one who is acquainted with the local conditions, it is an undisputed fact that if the Armenians of Van in April, 1915, by their heroic resistance had not kept busy that one division of regular Turkish troops and thousands of Kurds, and had made it possible for them to join the army of Khalil Bey, the Turks undoubtedly would have been able to crush the Russian forces in Persia and reach Baku in a few weeks, for the simple reason that from the banks of the Araxes to Baku the Russians had no forces at all, while the local Tartar inhabitants, armed and ready, were awaiting the coming of the Turks before rising en masse to join them. From the very be-

ANDRANIK
The commander of the first battalion of Armenian Volunteers

ginning of the war, Baku has been the real objective of the Turks, just as Paris has been the objective of the Germans, and that for two reasons: first, as a fountain of wealth, the Turks knew very well that the Russian government received from the oil wells of Baku an annual income of more than 200,000,000 rubles ($100,000,000), a sum which is more than all the revenues of the bankrupt Turkish government put together, and they looked upon these financial resources as indispensable for the accomplishment of their plan of a Pan-Turanian Empire; second, because the very plan of their Pan-Turanism had been introduced in Constantinople after 1908 by these very Tartars of Baku. The commanders of the Turkish forces engaged in Persia and Van— Khalil and Jevded—understood very well why their plans failed in the month of April, 1915; and that failure is the explanation of those frightful massacres which took place on the plains of Bitlis and Moush in June of the same year, when the armies of the same Khalil and Jevded, defeated in Persia and Van, were forced to retreat under the pressure of the Armenian volunteers.

The third Turkish offensive took place early in July, 1915. This time the Turks, with all their available forces—eleven divisions of regular troops, again under the command of Khalil Bey—attacked the very center of the Caucasian army. In a few days they re-occupied Malashkert, Toutakh, and the greater part of the plains of Alashkert. During one week the center of the Russian army retreated more than 100 kilometers (62 miles) leaving behind the district of Van entirely unprotected, and in danger of being surrounded at any moment. If the Turks had had one or two more divisions of troops at their service in those days, they would have been able very easily to take prisoners the entire fourth army of the Russian left wing and cut off their way of retreat. In order to escape from this dangerous situation, the Russian left wing was forced to retreat hastily toward the Russian frontier and sent a part of its forces to aid the central army. Only at the end of July did the Russian army, having received aid from its left wing, and under the leadership of the Armenian General Nazarbekoff, succeed in forcing back the Turks to their former line. These were the conditions under which nearly 150,000 Armenian inhabitants of the district of Van were compelled to leave all their property at the mercy of the enemy's fire and flee toward Erivan.

ARMENIAN RESISTANCE TO THE TURKISH MASSACRES

It is true that the battalions of Armenian volunteers took no active part in the battles of July, for they were then in the district of Van and undertaking the heavy duty of rear guard work for the Russian army and the Armenian refugees. But the Turkish Armenians behind the front, who were being deported and massacred as early as the month of July, by their heroic resistance, occupied the attention of four Turkish divisions and tens of thousands of Kurds just at the time when the Turks had such great need of those forces to aid them in their July drive. It is worth while, therefore, to point out here that, during the deportations and massacres of 1915, whenever the Armenians had any possible means at all of resisting the criminal plans of the Turkish government, they took up arms and organized resistance in different parts of Armenia.

Even before the deportations had begun, toward the latter part of 1914, the Turkish government cunningly attempted to disarm the Zeitunians, the brave Armenian mountaineers of Cilicia, who had taken up arms against the Turkish government at three different times in the nineteenth century, and each time had laid down their arms only on the intervention of the European powers, believing that they would put an end to the Turkish barbarities. This time the government filled the prisons with the prominent Zeitunians and persuaded the young warriors to surrender, promising to set them free if they did so. After accomplishing its deceitful plan, the government put to death most of the young men, deported the inhabitants, and made the mouhajirs from Balkans inhabit Zeitun, even changing the name of the place to Soulaymania, in order to erase the memory of those brave mountaineers. A group of warriors, however, found means to take up their arms, climb the mountains, and fight the Turkish soldiers. They are still free, and live among the mountains of Giaur Dagh. In the following year the inhabitants of Suediah were the first to defend themselves against the Turks. In April, when the Turkish government ordered the Armenian peasants of Suediah to leave their homes and emigrate toward Der-El-Zor, the inhabitants of four or five villages, nearly 5,000 in number, refused to obey this unlawful order of the Turkish government. With their families they climbed the Amanos mountains and for forty-two

Turkish cannons captured by the Armenians of Van in April, 1915.

days heroically resisted the cannonading of the regular Turkish forces. Their situation was of course critical. The desperate villagers sewed a large red cross on a white sheet to inform the fleet of the Allies in the Mediterranean that they were in danger. The French cruiser, Guechène, got in touch with the Armenian peasants, informed its war department of the situation, and obtained permission to remove them by transports to Port Said (Egypt). Most of them are still there, cared for by the British, while the young warriors went to join the French Oriental Legion, and fought on the Palestine front under General Allenby.

The resistance at Van has already been spoken of. The next place of importance must be given to the brave mountainous district of Sasoun, that very Sasoun which had retained its semi-independent position in Turkish Armenia up to the beginning of the last century, and had taken up arms at three different times in the present generation to defend its independence against the Ottoman troops—in 1894, in 1904, and again in 1915. This last time, toward the end of June, when the troops of Khalil and Jevded began to lay waste with fire and sword the city of Moush and the unprotected villages of the outlying district, the gallant Sasounians, under the guidance of their two idealistic leaders, came down from their mountains and made several raids on the city to drive away the Turks. One of their leaders was Roupen, a self-sacrificing and highly educated young man who had received his university training in Geneva, Switzerland, and had shouldered his gun in 1904 and had dedicated himself to the task of defending Sasoun. The name of the other was Vahan Papazian (a native of Van, but educated in Russian universities), who had been elected representative from Van to the Ottoman parliament. This daring step on the part of Sasoun forced the Turkish commanders to march on Sasoun with two divisions of troops and with nearly 30,000 Kurds. From the first days of July to Sept. 8, the Sasounians were able to resist the Turco-Kurdish attacks, always with the hope that the Russian army would come to their assistance. During that interval of time, the Sasounians sent several couriers to the Russian army and asked for help, but the Russian commanders remained indifferent, in spite of the fact that the extreme front line of the Russian army was scarcely 50 kilometers (31 miles) away from Sasoun, and the sound of the Turkish artillery aimed at the Sasounians could be heard very distinctly by the Russian army. One of the commanders of the Armenian volunteers, Dro, appealed to the Russian commander and asked for one battery of cannon and a score or two of machine guns, which would have enabled his men to break the Turkish front and join the Sasounians. That request likewise was refused by the heart-less commanders of despotic Russia. These were the conditions under which fell the historic Verdun of Armenia, heroic little Sasoun which, with its 10,000 mountaineers, succeeded in facing 50,000 Turks and Kurds for two months, with antiquated weapons and without adequate food or ammunition.

Making all due allowance for the relative magnitude and importance of the Near Eastern and the Western fronts, we may safely say without exaggeration that Van and Sasoun, on the Caucasian front in the year 1915, played exactly the same role which Liege played in 1914 and Verdun in 1916 on the Western front. Had it not been for these two points of stubborn resistance against the Turkish troops in the summer of 1915, the two Turkish offensives, already spoken of, would have had great chances of success. This is an undisputed fact with all the inhabitants of the Near East. And indeed, three months after these events, when the Armenian volunteers together with the Russian troops recommenced their drive and captured the cities of Moush and Bitlis, in the diary of a Turkish officer, who was taken prisoner in Bitlis, was found the following item, which appeared at the time in the Russian press:

"We are asked why we massacre the Armenians. The reason is quite plain to me. Had not the Armenians fought against us, we should have reached Tiflis and Baku long ago."

In addition to Van and Sasoun, during the same July when deportations and organized massacres were going on, three other places might be mentioned. where hopeless attempts at resistance were made by the Armenians against the savage Turks and Kurds. These places were Sivas, Urfa, and Shabin-Karahissar. At Sivas the heroic resistance of Mourat and his comrades and their escape were so full of thrilling events that they have been likened to the adventures of Odysseus. Mourat is a brave warrior who, together with his companion, Sepouh, had fought at Sasoun, in 1904, and had taken part in the Armenian and Tartar clashes of 1905 and 1906 in the Caucasus. When deportations

Dro

The commander of the second battalion of Armenian
volunteers.

and massacres commenced in 1915, Turkish gendarmes were sent to capture Mourat, who was living with his wife and child in a village near Sivas. Realizing the coming danger, Mourat climbed the mountains with his band of warriors and resisted the raids of the enemy. After a year and a half of stubborn resistance, he descended one day to the shore of the Black Sea, captured a Turkish sail-boat near Samsoun, and, putting his comrades into it, ordered the Turkish sailor to steer the boat toward Batoum, a Russian port. According to cable messages, Mourat was chased by a Turkish gun-boat. Several battles took place in which he lost a few of his men, but finally repulsed the Turks and reached Batoum safe and sound. At Urfa the Armenians were able for forty days to repulse the attacks of one Turkish division, but finally fell heroically under the fire of Turkish artillery, commanded by German officers, having previously destroyed all their property so that it would not fall into the hands of their enemies. In the ruined Armenian trenches at Urfa, by the side of Armenian young men there had fallen dead also Armenian young women who, arms in hand, were found all mangled by the German bombs. At Shabin-Karahissar, nearly 5,000 Armenians, for twenty-seven days without interruption, in the same month of July, kept busy another division of Turkish troops with their artillery. There took place one of the most tragic and heroic episodes of the present war. When the ammunition of the Armenians was almost gone, on the last day of the struggle, nearly 3,000 Armenian women and girls drank poison and died in order not to fall alive into the hands of the savage Turks. If the supply of poison had not given out, all the women would have done likewise. An eye-witness, one who had taken part in the struggle and who succeeded in reaching the Caucasus in 1916, after wandering in the mountains and valleys of Armenia for a whole year, related how on that last day Armenian mothers and girls, with tears in their eyes and with hymns on their lips, received poison from the Armenian physicians and apothecaries for themselves and their little ones. When the supply of poison gave out, those who were unable to obtain any uttered terrible wailing, and many of the girls cast themselves down from the rocks of the Karahissar citadel and committed suicide.

These events reveal the following facts: first, that in spite of all the precautions which the Turkish government employed to disarm the Armenians before carrying out its fiendish design, the Armenians found means to organize in the four corners of Armenia hopeless but serious plans of resistance against the swords of their enemy; second, that in order to eliminate these Armenian points of resistance during the summer of 1915, five Turkish divisions and tens of thousands of Kurds were kept employed, and were unable to add their immediate co-operation in those very days to the other Turkish forces engaged in their two offensives on the Caucasian front. These were the positive services which the martyred Armenian people rendered to the allied cause in the Near East. Their active resistance to the Turco-German plans, however, cost the Armenians more than one million men massacred under the most savage conditions, and the deprivation of their means of livelihood in Turkish Armenia. But, to complete the description of the Armenian Calvary, it is necessary to picture also in a few words the attitude assumed by the government of the Russian Czar toward the very Armenian people whose active participation on Russia's side enabled the Caucasian front to repulse the Turkish attacks in 1914 and 1915, and, moreover, to accomplish definite successes during the following year, 1916.

ATTITUDE OF RUSSIAN CZARISM TOWARD THE ARMENIANS

As we have already mentioned, from the beginning of the war the Russian bureaucracy tried on the one hand by various false promises to win over the sympathy of the Armenians, while on the other it tried by every means to keep the Armenian military forces away from the Caucasian front. Only seven battalions of Armenian volunteers were kept on the Caucasian front. As we have already seen, those few battalions even, in 1914 and 1915, rendered to the Russians invaluable services, twice saving the right and left wings of the Russian army from an unavoidable catastrophe by their heroic resistance; but the Russian official communiqués do not contain one line in which the battalions of Armenian volunteers are even mentioned. The same silence was maintained by the Russian communiqués concerning the heroic resistance of the Armenians at Van, and with regard to the assistance which the Armenian volunteers rushed to that city. This was the policy of the government of Russian Czarism from the beginning of the war to the end of its existence,—to avoid in every way

The civilian Armenians of Urfa who defended themselves against the Turks and the Kurds in July, 1915.

speaking about the Armenians and Armenia. The Russian press was even forbidden to speak about the massacres carried on in Turkish Armenia at the hands of the Turkish government. Therefore, when the capture of Erzeroum in 1916 made the immediate co-operation of the Armenian volunteers unnecessary to the Russians, the commander-in-chief of the Caucasian army at the time, Grand Duke Nicolas Nicolaevitch, ordered the disbanding of all the battalions of the Armenian volunteers. Besides this amazing treatment of the Armenian military forces, the Czar's government removed from the Caucasus before the war all the Armenian officers and replaced them by generals (manifestly anti-Armenian in spirit) from the Russians, Georgians, and other Caucasian races. The object of this move was to enable the government to check the national aspirations of the Armenians, and to give it a plausible opportunity at the end of the war to take over the Armenian vilayets without gratifying the demands of the Armenians for autonomy.

From the third month of the war, it became clear to us that the Russian government pursued unswervingly its Lobanoff-policy toward the Armenians. What was that policy? In 1896, when an English correspondent interviewed the Russian minister of foreign affairs, Count Lobanoff Rostowsky, and asked him why Russia did not occupy the Armenian vilayets of Turkey in order to save that Christian people from the Turkish massacres, the Russian minister cynically replied: "We need Armenia, but without the Armenians." It is worth while, then, to give here a few actual facts which reveal this fiendish policy pursued by the Russian government toward a people which was the only one of all the peoples of the Caucasus and the Near East to help the Russian army by its unreserved co-operation, and which was the only factor that saved the Caucasian front from an unavoidable catastrophe in 1914 and 1915.

ONE. Every time that the Russian army was forced to retreat from the recaptured parts of Turkish Armenia, no precautionary measures were taken in order to save the local Armenian inhabitants from the inevitable massacres. For example, in December, 1914, when the Turks advanced as far as Sarikamish and Ardahan and forced the central Russian army to retreat from the neighborhood of Alashkert and Bayazid, the commander of the local forces, General Abatzieff (an Acétine Moslem who had joined the Greek church) strictly ordered the local Armenian inhabitants, nearly 32,000 in number, not to stir from their places, and in order to have his command accurately carried out he placed mounted Cossack patrols in the plains of Alashkert lest the Armenian peasants should emigrate toward the Russian frontier, in which direction the Russian army with its transports had already been moving since December 13. Three days later the second battalion of the Armenian volunteers, which had been fighting in the first-line positions for over two months under the command of the same general, returned to the army headquarters for a well-earned rest, and there only it heard about the serious happenings already mentioned, and the extraordinary attitude assumed by the Russian general. The Armenian peasants from every side appealed to the Armenian volunteers with tears in their eyes and begged to be saved from an inevitable massacre. The commander of the Armenian volunteers, Armen Garo, and his brave assistant, Khetcho, who died like a hero in July, 1915, on the shores of Lake Van, went immediately to General Abatzieff and asked him to revoke his order and permit the Armenian inhabitants to move with the army toward Igdir. The hostile general refused their request, his answer being that, if the people stirred from the place, he would be unable to remove the army transports soon enough. When he heard this answer, Armen Garo immediately telegraphed to Igdir and appealed to the commander-in-chief of the fourth army, General Oganowsky, and in touching words asked for his intervention. On the following day only, thanks to the intervention of General Oganowsky, the Armenian volunteers received permission to organize the retreat of the Armenian inhabitants of the plains of Alashkert toward Igdir and to defend them from the attacks of the Kurds. During the seven days that the retreat lasted the Armenians lost only 400 persons, and most of those on account of the severe cold. Another example of this hostile treatment of the Armenians by the Russian authorities might be mentioned,—the retreat from the Van district in July, 1915. There General Nikolaeff for eight continuous days deceived the Armenian leaders and made them remain idle (telling them every day that he would not retreat under any circumstances, and that therefore it was entirely needless to remove the people), until behold, one day, July 18, he suddenly sent for the mayor of Van, Aram, and the commander-in-chief of the Armenian volunteers, Vartan, and informed them that he had received

KHETCHO

The commander of the cavalry corps of the Armenian
volunteers, who was killed in July, 1915, near Bitlis.

orders to retreat immediately, but in order to make it possible for the people to prepare for departure, he would wait until the 20th of the month. Thus the Armenian leaders were forced to remove in two or three days nearly 150,000 people of the Van region, and if those three battalions of Armenian volunteers had not been there to protect the people from Kurdish and Turkish raids, the loss of life during the journey would have been tenfold more than it actually was. Whereas, if the Russian general had not been so deceitful in his behavior but had given an opportunity of seven or eight days to organize the retreat, it would have been possible to direct the people to Erivan without the loss of a single life. The Armenians suffered a loss of 8,000 to 10,000 men, women, and children during the retreat.

Two. When Turkish Armenia was almost wholly emptied of its Armenian inhabitants, due to these successive retreats, the Russian government raised all sorts of barriers before the refugees to prevent them from returning to their former homes when the Russian army recaptured the Armenian vilayets. For example, in 1916-1917, scarcely 8,000 to 10,000 Armenians were permitted to go back and inhabit the region of Van; the rest were compelled to stay within the borders of the Caucasus as refugees. Toward the latter part of 1916, even among Russian governmental circles there was talk of transferring to Siberia nearly 250,000 Turkish Armenian immigrants who had sought refuge in the Caucasus, because it was objected that no available lands existed there for them. Russians considered it a settled question that even after the war the Turkish Armenians would not be permitted to return to their own homes.

On the other hand, the same Russian bureaucracy resorted to every means to win the sympathy of the Turkish and Kurdish inhabitants remaining in Armenia. With that purpose in view, in the spring of 1916, on behalf of the ministry for foreign affairs at Petrograd, Count Chakhowsky with his own organization established himself in Bashkalé (a city in the district of Van) and distributed nearly 24,000 rifles to the Kurds of the neighboring regions. It is needless to say that not long after those very rifles were used by the Kurds against the Russian army both in Persia and Armenia. This amazing action of Count Chakhowsky was taken so openly that it was even known to ordinary Russian soldiers, who were extremely enraged against the Count, a fact which accounts for the murder of the same Count Chakhowsky in Persia by Russian soldiers, when the discipline of the Russian army was relaxed on account of the revolution which took place in the spring of 1917.

THREE. While the Russians were preventing the Turkish Armenian immigrants from returning to their own lands, they, in the spring of 1916, commenced to organize in Turkish Armenia colonies of Cossacks. The Russian administration sent special propagandists to the northern Caucasus to persuade the Cossacks living there to move to Armenia, and during that same year 5,000 of them, under the name of agricultural battalions, were already cultivating the plains of Alashkert, lands which rightly belonged to the Armenians. This last act of the Russian government was so revolting that even the liberal organs of the Russian press complained of the government for such inhuman proceedings, while in the Russian Duma two Russian representatives, N. Milukoff and A. Kerensky (both of whom played such great roles the following year in the downfall of Czarism), publicly criticised the government of the Czar for its base treatment of the Armenians. Documentary evidence relating to this disgraceful action of the Russian government, which incensed the ire of prominent liberals in the Duma, may be found in the July 28, 1916, issue of the *Retch*, the organ of the Constitutional Democrats in Russia. In order to characterize this criminal action of the Russian bureaucracy against the Armenian people who were martyred for the allied cause, it may be worth while also to cite the following details:

In the month of July, 1915, the Armenian inhabitants of Erzeroum, nearly 25,000 in number, were likewise deported by the Turkish government, leaving all their real and personal property at the disposal of the Turks. The governor of the place, Tahsin Bey, arranged a scheme by means of which every Armenian before leaving the city could store his goods and household furniture (with the name of the owner on each article) in the cathedral, with the apparent purpose of returning them to their owners after the war, but with the real purpose of preventing so much riches from falling into the hands of the Turkish mob, in order to appropriate them later for the government. The cathedral of Erzeroum was packed with the goods of the exiled Armenians when the Russians captured the city in February, 1916. Ordinary human decency demanded that the Russians should not

The mounted troops of the second battalion of Armenian volunteers of the Caucasus, November, 1914.

have touched the articles stored in that sacred edifice, especially as they belonged to the very martyred people whose professed sympathies for them (the Russians) were the cause of their being exiled to the deserts of Mesopotamia. But the fact is that the commander of the Russian army, General Kaledine himself, set the example of desecration; he personally entered the cathedral first, and selected for himself a few car-loads of rugs and sundry valuable articles. Then the other officers of the Russian army followed his example, and in a few days half of the contents of the church was already pillaged before the representative of the Armenian Committee, Mr. Rostom, after repeated telegrams, was able to receive an order from Tiflis to stop the plunder. In that same summer of 1916, the Buxton brothers (representatives of the Armenian Committee of London) and other English Armenophiles came to Armenia. When they witnessed all these disgraceful particulars they could not believe their own eyes, so monstrous was the attitude of the Russian government toward the Armenians. The English and American friends of Armenia consoled them by saying that on their return they would have the privilege of explaining this state of affairs to their government and that they would doubtless do all in their power to protect the rights of the Armenians. These were the circumstances under which the Armenian people joined its fate to the allied cause from the very beginning of the war, and, having made colossal sacrifices during three whole years, was almost crushed to death in the claws of Turkish and Russian despotism.

In that same sorrowful summer of 1916 the Armenians heard the news that England, France, and Russia had signed an agreement concerning Armenia. According to that agreement Russia was to take over the three vilayets of Turkish Armenia, Erzeroum, Bitlis, and Van, while southern Armenia and Cilicia were to be put under the guardianship of France. One must be an Armenian in order to feel the depth and intensity of the bitterness and disappointment which filled the hearts of all the wandering Armenians from the Caucasus to Mesopotamia. Every Armenian asked himself or herself: Was this to be our recompense?

In those very days (September, 1916) one of the agents of the German government in Switzerland approached Dr. Zavrieff (one of the representatives of the Armenian Committee of that place) with the following proposal:

"You Armenians made a great mistake when you joined your fate to that of the Allies. It is time for you to rectify your mistaken policy. Your dreams with regard to the historic Armenia are unrealizable. You may as well accustom yourselves to that fact, and before it is too late you will do better to join the fate of your people with the German policies, and remove the remnants of the Armenian people to Mesopotamia, where the Germans will put at the disposal of the Armenians every means which will enable them to create for themselves a new and a more fortunate fatherland under their (German) immediate protection."

In order to persuade his Armenian opponent, the German agent constantly reminded him of the agreement (between England, France and Russia), and especially of the hostile attitude of the Russians up to that time towards the Armenians. The news of this German proposal reached the Caucasus in December of the same year. It was made the subject of serious consultation among the Armenian leaders. The writer of these lines was present at those conferences, and his impression was this: Had there not been that superhuman adoration (so peculiarly Armenian) which every Armenian has for his ancestral home and recollections so sanctified by blood, the German proposal would very likely have been accepted by the Armenians at that psychological moment when their hearts were overflowing with bitterness and disappointment toward the Russian government,—a member of the allied nations. The outcome of those conferences was that we decided to continue our former policy toward the Entente, in spite of the base behavior of the Russians towards us, and at the same time to invite the serious attention of our great Allies of the west to our hopeless situation.

ROLE PLAYED BY THE ARMENIANS IN THE CAUCASUS
AFTER THE RUSSIAN COLLAPSE.

This was the state of affairs when there came the crash of the Russian revolution. The heart of every Armenian was greatly relieved, thinking that the greater part of their torments would come to an end. And in truth, during the first few months of the revolution, the temporary government of Kerensky made definite arrangements to rectify the unjust treatment of the Armenians by the government of the Czar. But events progressed in a precipitate manner. The demoralization of the

KHETCHO   DRO   ARMEN GARO

The staff of the second battalion of Armenian volunteers in the Caucasus in November, 1914.

Russian troops on all the fronts assumed greater proportions as the days went by. Foreseeing the danger which threatened the Caucasus, the Armenian National Organization of the Caucasus, as early as April, 1917, sent to Petrograd on a special mission Dr. Zavrieff, already mentioned, and the writer of these lines, in order to have them obtain permission to transfer to the Caucasus some 150,000 Armenian officers and men (scattered throughout the Russian army), by whose assistance the Armenians might be able to protect their own native land against the Turkish advance. Mr. Kerensky, who was well acquainted with the abnormal conditions reigning in the Caucasus, agreed to grant the request of the Armenian delegates, but, on the other hand, for fear of receiving similar requests from the other races in case he granted an order favorable to the Armenians, he decided to fulfill our request unofficially, that is, without a general ordinance, to send the Armenian soldiers to the Caucasus gradually, in small groups, in order not to attract the attention of the other races. And he carried out this plan.

But unfortunately, scarcely 35,000 Armenian soldiers had been able to reach the Caucasus by November, 1917, when Kerensky himself fell at the hands of the Bolsheviks, and there was created a chaotic condition the result of which was the final demobilization of the Russian army. During December, 1917, and January, 1918, the Russian army of 250,000 men on the Caucasian front, without any orders, abandoned its positions and moved into the interior of Russia, leaving entirely unprotected a front about 970 kilometers (600 miles) in length, extending from the Black Sea to Persia. As soon as the Russian army disbanded, the 3,000,000 Tartar inhabitants of the Caucasus armed themselves and rose en masse. Toward the end of January last, the Tartars had cut the Baku-Tiflis railroad line as well as the Erivan-Joulfa line, and now began to raid and plunder the Armenian cities and villages, while behind, on the frontier, the regular Turkish army had commenced to advance in the first days of February. Against all these Turks and Tartars the Armenians had one army corps made up of some 35,000 regular troops under the command of General Nazarbekoff, and nearly 20,000 Armenian volunteers under the command of their experienced leaders. Armenia's only hope of assistance was their neighbors, the Georgians, who were as much interested in the protection of the Caucasus as the Armenians were, because the Turkish demands of the Brest-Litovsk treaty included definite portions of Georgia, as well as of Armenia; for example, the port of Batoum. And in fact, during the months of January and February they seemed quite inclined to help the Armenians, but when the Turks captured Batoum on April 15 and came as far as Usurgeti, the morale of the Georgians was completely broken, and they immediately sent a delegation to Berlin and put Georgia under German protection. From this time on the 2,000,000 Armenian inhabitants of the Caucasus remained entirely alone to face, on the one hand, the Turkish regular army of 100,000 men, and on the other hand, the armed forces of hundreds of thousands of Tartars. From the end of February the small number of Armenian forces commenced to retreat step by step before the superior Turkish forces, from Erzingan, Baiburt, Khenous, Mamakhatoun, Erzeroum, and Bayazid, and concentrated their forces on the former Russian-Turkish frontier. Here commenced serious battles which arrested for quite a long time the advance of the Turkish troops. It took them until April 22 to arrive before the forts of Kars, where the first serious resistance of the Armenians took place. The fierce Turkish attack which continued for four days was easily repulsed by the Armenians, owing to the guns on the ramparts of Kars.

During these events a temporary government of the Caucasus existed in Tiflis, composed of representatives of three Caucasian races—Georgian, Armenian, and Tartar. This Caucasian government was formed immediately after the *coup d'etat* of the Bolsheviks, and conducted Caucasian affairs as an independent body. It refused to recognize the authority of the Bolshevik government, or the terms of the Brest-Litovsk treaty signed by its accredited delegates. The president of the government was Chekhenkeli, a Georgian. Immediately after the capture of Batoum the Caucasian government opened peace negotiations with Turkish delegates in Batoum itself. The Turks, by their usual crafty tricks, persuaded the Georgian delegates that they would return Batoum to the Georgians if Kars surrendered without resistance. Feeling assured of this Turkish promise, the Georgian president of the Caucasian government, Chekhenkeli, on the night of April 25, without consultation with the other members of the government, telegraphed the commander of Kars that an armistice had been signed with the Turks on condition of surrendering Kars, and therefore to give up the

MOURAT

Who lead the volunteers at Erzingan after the Russian collapse and died
heroically in the fighting at Baku.

forts immediately and retreat as far as Arpa-Chai. On the following day the commander of the Armenian soldiers who were defending Kars delivered the fortress into the hands of the Turks and retreated to Alexandropol. Then it became known that Chekhenkeli had sent the fateful telegram on his own responsibility, but it was already too late. This event occasioned very strained relations between the Armenians and Georgians. Not long after, on the 26th of May, the Georgians, assured of German protection, declared in Tiflis the independence of Georgia. Thus the temporary Caucasian government dissolved.

After the separation of the Georgians the Armenian National Council of the Caucasus declared Armenian independence, under the name of the Republic of Ararat, with Erivan as its capital. While the negotiations were going on in Batoum—always between the delegates of the Turks and the three Caucasian races comprising the Caucasian temporary government,—the Turkish armies, after the occupation of Kars, became more aggressive and commenced to advance toward Alexandropol and Karakilissa. Concentrating their forces around Karakilissa and Erivan, early in June, the Armenians in two fierce battles drove the Turks back almost to their frontier. In the battle of Karakilissa, which lasted four days, the Turks left 6,000 dead before the Armenian posts, and escaped to Alexandropol. When the Turks felt that their position in the face of the Armenian resistance was becoming more and more hopeless and that it would cost them dear to continue the fight, they immediately began to make concessions. Up to that time the Turks had not yet recognized the right of Russian Armenia to independence, their objection being that they only recognized in the Caucasus Georgian and Tartar countries. But when they heard the news of the last military victory of the Armenians, on June 14, in Batoum, the Turkish delegates, together with the representatives of the Republic of Ararat, signed the first terms of armistice, leaving the final peace signature to the congress of Constantinople, where the final negotiations were to take place.

The delegates of the three nations of the Caucasus reached Constantinople on June 19. They were 32 in number. Among them were also the representatives of the Republic of Ararat, Mr. A. Khatissoff, the minister of foreign affairs, and Mr. A. Aharonian, the president of the Armenian National Council. In that congress, which convened in presence of the delegates of the German and Austrian governments, the Turks signed peace treaties with each of the newly-formed Caucasian Republics. It is needless to say that those treaties had as much value as that which the Roumanian government was forced to sign a few months before by the central powers. And, as was expected, the Turks and the Germans rewarded the Georgians and the Tartars at the expense of the Armenians. They gave the greater part of the Armenian territories to the other two nations, and the remainder was claimed by Turkey, with the exception of 32,000 square kilometers (about 12,350 square miles), with 700,000 Armenian inhabitants, which were left to the Republic of Ararat. According to these terms only one-third of the Armenians of the Caucasus are included within the Republic of Ararat, while the remaining 1,400,000 Armenians are left in territories allotted to the Tartars or the Georgians.

That portion of the Armenians which inhabits the mountainous regions of Karabagh (which was assigned to the Tartars), up to this very day, October, 1918, resists the Turco-Tartar hordes and refuses at any price to be subjected to the unjust terms of the treaty of Constantinople, while beyond, the Armenians at Van, when their military forces realized that their retreat was cut off early last May, after being sheltered for two whole months in Van, moved toward Persia, there joined the Christian Assyrians in the neighborhood of Urmia, repulsed for a long time the Turkish and Kurdish attacks, and only early in September succeeded in shattering the Turkish lines and thereby reached the city of Hamadan in Persia, where they entrusted to the care of the British forces the protection of about 40,000 Armenian and Assyrian refugees. In order to complete this picture of the heroic resistance of the Caucasian Armenians, let me say a few words more about the struggle at Baku.

As already mentioned, early in May, 1917, through the efforts of the Armenian National Organization of the Caucasus, the Armenian soldiers and officers scattered throughout Russia were gradually brought together and mobilized on the Caucasian front. With that purpose in view an Armenian Military Committee was formed in Petrograd with General Bagradouni as president. Bagradouni was one of the most brilliant young generals of the Russian army. He had received his military training at the highest military academy of Petrograd, and, during Kerensky's administration, was appointed Chief of the Staff of the military

Armenians valiantly defending Baku against the Tartars.

Taken from "Asia."

forces at Petrograd. When the Bolsheviks assumed power they ordered him to take an oath of loyalty to the new government. General Bagradouni refused to do so, and for that reason he was imprisoned, with many other high military officials. After remaining in prison two months, through repeated appeals by the Armenian National bodies, he was freed by the Bolsheviks on condition that he should immediately leave Petrograd. After his release from prison, General Bagradouni, accompanied by the well known Armenian social worker, Mr. Rostom, with 200 Armenian officers, left for the Caucasus to assume the duties of commander-in-chief of the newly-formed Armenian army. This group of Armenian officers reached Baku early in March, where it was forced to wait, for the simple reason that the Baku-Tiflis railroad line was already cut by the Tartars. During that same month of March from many parts of Russia a large number of Armenians gathered at Baku and waited to go to Erivan and Tiflis in response to the call issued by the Armenian National Council. Toward the end of March nearly 110,000 Armenian soldiers had come together at Baku.

By the 30th of March the news of German victories was spread throughout the Caucasus by the Turco-German agents. On the same day in Baku and other places appeared the following leaflets:

"Awake, Turkish brothers!

"Protect your rights; union with the Turks means life.

"Unite, O Children of the Turks!

"Brothers of the noble Turkish nation, for hundreds of years our blood has flowed like water, our motherland has been ruined, and we have been under the heel of thousands of oppressors who have almost crushed us. We have forgotten our nation. We do not know to whom to appeal for help.

"Countrymen, we consider ourselves free hereafter. Let us look into our conscience! Let us not listen to the voice of plotters. We must not lose the way to freedom; our freedom lies in union with the Turks. It is necessary for us to unite and put ourselves under the protection of the Turkish flag.

"Forward, brothers! Let us gather ourselves under the flag of union and stretch out our hands to our Turkish brothers. Long life to the generous Turkish nation! By these words we shall never again bear a foreign yoke, the chains of servitude."

And on the following day (March 31) from all sides of the Caucasus the armed hordes of Tartars attacked the Armenians. The leaders of the Tartars at Baku were convinced that they would easily disarm the Armenian soldiers, because they were somewhat shut up in Baku, but they were sadly mistaken in their calculations. After a bloody battle which lasted a whole week the Armenians remained masters of the city and its oil wells. They suffered a loss of nearly 2,500 killed, while the Tartars lost more than 10,000. The commander of the military forces of the Armenians was the same General Bagradouni, who, although he lost both of his legs during the fight, continued his duties until September 14, when the Armenians and the small number of Englishmen who came to their assistance were forced to abandon Baku to the superior forces of the Turco-Tartars, and retreat toward the city of Enzeli in the northern Caucasus.

During these heroic struggles, which lasted five and a half months, the small Armenian garrison of Baku, together with a few thousand Russians, defended Baku and its oil wells against tens of thousands of Tartars, the Caucasian mountaineers, and more than one division of regular Turkish troops which had come to the assistance of the latter by way of Batoum. Time after time the Turkish troops made fierce attacks to capture the city, but each time they were repulsed with heavy losses by the gallant Armenian garrison. The Armenians had built their hopes on British assistance, since nothing was expected from the demoralized Russian army. But, unfortunately, the British were unable to reach Baku with large forces from their Bagdad army. Nevertheless, on August 5, they landed at Baku 2,800 men to help the Armenians. The arrival of this small British contingent caused great enthusiasm among the tired and exhausted defenders of the city. But meanwhile the Turks had received new forces from Batoum and renewed their attacks. After a series of bloody battles the armed Armenian and British forces were forced to leave Baku on September 14 and retreat toward Persia, taking with them nearly 10,000 refugees from the inhabitants of the city. As to the condition of those who were left behind, this much is certain; that on the day the city was occupied by the Turco-Tartars, nearly 20,000 Armenians were put to the sword, the greater portion of them being women and children. According to the news received from Persia, after that first terrible massacre, other

Young Armenian students in France, who took part in the immortal defence of Verdun in 1916.

massacres likewise have taken place. The number of the losses is not known; but it may safely be surmised without any exaggeration that out of the entire 80,000 Armenian inhabitants of Baku, all those who were unable to leave the city in time were slaughtered by the revengeful Turks and Tartars. Thus ended the resistance of five months and a half by the Armenians at Baku against the Turco-Germans.

The remnants of the retreating Armenian garrison of Baku, at the time of writing, are located in the Persian city of Enzeli, where, under the command of their heroic leader, General Bagradouni, they are recuperating before hastening to the aid of the Armenians in the eastern Caucasus, who, as already mentioned, up to this very day are resisting the forces of the Turco-Tartars in the mountains of Karabagh.

Armenia's Co-operation With the Allies on Other Fronts.

The Armenians, besides battling on the Caucasian front, where they have been fighting in their own native land, have co-operated unreservedly with the Allies on far distant fronts, as for example on the French front. At the beginning of the war the young Armenian students living in France—about 900 in number—volunteered to serve in the French army for the defence of civilization and freedom. Today, scarcely 50 of them are alive; the majority of the 850 others gave their lives in 1916 in the immortal defence of Verdun. This small episode in this universal drama will not be forgotten by either France or the Free Armenia of the future. Glory to the memory of those immortal heroes! Beyond, on another front of the war, by an extraordinary coincidence of fate, in the deadly blow which fell on the head of the criminal Ottoman Empire in the Holy Land, the sons of the sorrowful people whom it had ruthlessly slaughtered had their just share of active participation. And indeed, in General Allenby's victorious army, which saved Palestine and Syria from Turkish tyranny in September, 1918, by General Allenby's own testimony, the eight battalions of the Armenian volunteers (who took part in those battles under the French flag) were conspicuous for their bravery. In response to a congratulatory telegram from the chairman of the Armenian National Union of Egypt for the victories on the Palestine front, General Allenby said: "I thank you warmly for your congratulations, and am proud of the fact that your Armenian compatriots in the Oriental Legion took an active part in the fighting and shared in our victory."

CONCLUSION.

If we wish to condense all we have said in a few pages, we shall have the following picture:

In 1914 both Turkey and Russia appealed to the Armenians by various promises of a future autonomous Armenia to secure their assistance in their respective military operations. Through their long and bitter experience the Armenians knew very well that the imperialistic governments of both Turkey and of Russia were opposed to their national aspirations and therefore those promises had no value whatever. But, realizing the universal significance of the present war, and considering the fact that justice was on the side of the Entente, the Armenians, in spite of their distrust of the Russian government, from the very beginning, unreservedly bound themselves to the allied cause.

This decision of the Armenians cost them the sacrifice of more than 1,000,000 men in Turkish Armenia, and complete devastation of their native land even in the first year of the war.

In spite of this terrible blow, the Armenians did not lose their vigor, and, even though the autocratic Russian government, up to the time of the Revolution, created all sorts of obstacles to impede their activities, they still continued their assistance to the allied cause. In bringing about the failure of the three Turkish offensives in 1914 and 1915 the Armenians gave the allied cause important armed assistance, on both sides of the Turco-Russian frontier.

After the Russian Revolution, when, the Russian military forces fled from the Caucasian front and left it unprotected from January, 1918, to the middle of the following September, the Armenians were the only people who resisted and delayed the Turco-German advance toward Baku. Moreover, the Armenians accomplished all this with their own forces, all alone, surrounded on all sides by hostile elements, without any means of communication with their great Allies of the West. As an evidence of this we may mention the fact that during the last eight

Armenian volunteers who fought on the Palestine front in September and October, 1918, under the command of Gen. Allenby.

months and a half the Armenians have received from the Allies only 6,500,000 rubles ($3,250,000) of financial assistance, and the 2,800 British soldiers who were too few and arrived too late to save Baku.

Let us now look at the other side of the picture.

Had the Armenians assumed an entirely opposite attitude from what they actually did; in other words, had they bound their fate in 1914 to the Turco-German cause, just as the Bulgarians did in 1915, what would have been the trend of events in the Near East? Here is a question to which, it is quite possible, our great Allies have had no time to give any consideration. But that very question was put before the Armenians in 1914, and with no light heart did they answer it by their decision to join the Allies. Each and every one of them had a clear presentiment of the terrible responsibility they assumed. Those millions of corpses of Armenian women and children which spotted the plains in the summer of 1915, rose like phantoms before our very eyes in the August of 1914 when we decided to resist the wild Turkish revengefulness and its frightful outcome. Now, in October, 1918, when we are so close to the hour of the final victory, and feel quite safe and certain that the heavy and gloomy days of the summer of 1914 will never return, I shall permit myself to picture in a few words, before I finish, that which would have taken place if the Armenians had sided with the Germano-Turks in the Near East from the beginning of the war.

First of all, those frightful Armenian massacres would not have taken place. On the contrary, the Turks and the Germans would have tried to win the sympathy of the Armenians in every possible way until the end of the war.

On the other hand, so long as the Georgians and Tartars of the Caucasian peoples were only too eager to co-operate with the Germano-Turks, as the events of 1918 fully demonstrate, had the Armenians likewise joined them in 1914, by cutting the railroads, the backbone of the Caucasian Russian army, all the Caucasian country would have slipped out of the hands of the Russians in a few weeks, and the Turco-Germans would have reached Baku in the autumn of the same year. The Armenians, Georgians, and Tartars of the Caucasus, united, would have been able to form with the greatest ease an army of 700,000 men, by which they would have been able to defend the Caucasian mountain-ridge against the Russians. Meanwhile, the entire Turkish army would have been available to advance immediately toward the interior of Asia and join the 18,000,000 Moslems of Asiatic Russia. We may safely say, neither Persia nor Afghanistan could have remained neutral on seeing such successful achievements by the Turks.

In the course of such events Russia would have been compelled to remove the greater portion of her forces to the East and would not have been able to protect her Western frontiers as successfully as she did. Therefore, quite probably, the Russian collapse would have taken place in the summer of 1915, when the Germans occupied Russian Poland. On the other hand, Great Britain would have been obliged to appropriate the greater portion of her newly-formed land forces for the protection of India, and would have been unable to rush as great a force to the defence of heroic France as she actually did. Quite likely, under these conditions, neither Italy nor Roumania would have abandoned her neutrality, and thus the war might have ended in 1915 or 1916 with the victory of the central Powers, at least on land.

It was as clear as day to the Armenians that a Germano-Turkish victory could never satisfy their national aspirations. The most that those nations would have done for us would have been to grant nominal rights to the Armenia of their own choice. But it was very plain to us also that we should not have suffered such frightful human losses had we not sided with the Allies. We consciously chose this last alternative, namely: we tied our fate to the allied victory; we exposed our very existence to danger in order to realize the complete fulfillment of our national ambition, that is, to see the re-establishment of the United Historic Independent Armenia.

With our modest means, we have fulfilled our duty in full measure in this great struggle in order to save civilization from an impending doom. Now it is for our great Allies to act.

The day is not very far distant when, gathered around the great tribunal of justice, the representatives of all the nations of the globe—guilty or just—are to receive their punishment or reward from the hands of the four distinguished champions of democracy, President Wilson, Premiers Lloyd George, Georges Clemenceau, and Orlando. If the representatives present themselves in the order of seniority, the first in the rank will be the representative of the Armenian people—the aged Mother Armenia. Behold! Into the Peace Congress Hall there enters an old woman, bathed in blood, clothed in rags, her face covered with wrinkles 3,000 years old, and completely exhausted. With her thoughtful eyes the venerable Mother Armenia will survey the countenances of all those present, and thus will she address the great figures of the world:

"Century after century my sons took part in all the strifes waged to safeguard justice and the freedom of suffering humanity. Three thousand years ago my sons struggled for seven hundred years against the despotism of Babylon and Nineveh, which eventually collapsed under the load of their own crimes. Fifteen centuries ago the Armenians resisted for five hundred years the persecutions of the mighty Persian Empire to preserve their Christian faith. Since the eighth century my sons have been the vanguard of Christian civilization in the East against Moslem invasions threatening for a while the very existence of all Europe. If you doubt my statements, ask the sacred mountain of Ararat; he will relate to you how all the nations and empires, which attempted to possess by criminal means the indisputable inheritance of my sons, have received their just punishment.

"Let us not go very far. Here, before you, stand the representatives of those three nations which tried to destroy my sons before your very eyes, in order to rule those parts of our ancestral lands, so sanctified by blood, known as Armenia. Look at this Turk; it was he who wished to wipe the very name of Armenia off the face of the map; but today, foiled in his attempt, he stands there like a criminal awaiting his sentence. And where is today the Czar of Russia, who planned to occupy Armenia without the Armenians,—the representative of that Empire before which the world trembled. And what has remained of the policies of the German Empire, in whose hands is the Bagdad railroad now, built at the cost of the blood of hundreds of thousands of Armenian women and children? Thus, those three modern malevolent empires, which tried to attain happiness through the blood of my sons, have received their just punishment.

"Such will be the fate in the future of all those who shall attempt similar crimes against Armenia. This is the message, gentlemen, handed down to us through three thousand years of history.

"I have nothing more to add. I await your verdict with confidence."

CPSIA information can be obtained at www.ICGtesting.com
Printed in the USA
BVOW06s0436241214

380743BV00004B/106/P